Born Free Foundation's
Wild About Animals

Born Free Foundation's
Wild About Animals

A Collection of Children's Poems about Animals

Paws n Claws Publishing ©
Using the written word to keep animals in the wild

Featuring Winning Poems from
Born Free Foundation's 30th Anniversary
Children's Poetry Competition

PAWS N CLAWS PUBLISHING
Paws n Claws Publishing, Canvey Island, Essex
www.pawsnclawspublishing.co.uk

Edited by Debz Hobbs-Wyatt
Designed and Typeset by Martin James

British Library Cataloguing in Publication Data
A Record of this Publication is available from the
British Library

ISBN 978-0-9568939-8-7

Acknowledgements

A huge thank you to all those who gave their time to this special anniversary project for the Born Free Foundation. From the team of lovely judges – Pam Ayres, Brian Patten, Lauren St John, Richard Bonfield, Virginia McKenna and Debz Hobbs-Wyatt, to our typesetter who gave us his skills and time for free, Martin James, on loan from Bridge House Publishing, without whom you would not be holding or viewing this lovely book. And of course to all of you for sending us your poems and drawings or for simply supporting the project by buying a copy of the book.

Nothing like this is possible without a dedicated team so thank you to everyone involved!

The Born Free Foundation is an international wildlife charity founded by Virginia McKenna, Bill Travers and their eldest son Will Travers, following Bill and Virginia's starring roles in the classic film *Born Free*. Today, headed by Will, the Foundation is devoted to wild animal welfare and compassionate conservation, working to save animal lives, stop suffering, rescue individuals and protect rare species. Our charity is determined to end captive animal exploitation, phase out zoos and keep wildlife in the wild. We take action for lions, elephants, gorillas, tigers, wolves, bears, dolphins, turtles and many other species, and work with local communities to find solutions to help people and wildlife live together without conflict.

Find out more and get involved at www.bornfree.org.uk

Born Free Foundation
Broadlands Business Campus, Langhurstwood Road, Horsham, West Sussex, RH12 4QP, UK
Charity Reg. No. 1070906

Contents

7

9

10

Foreword

It was with the mixed emotions of astonishment and delight that I read all the poems sent to us by the children who entered the Born Free competition. I have to admit that I was taken aback by the perception and sensitivity of these young writers, and filled with admiration for their poetic skills.

Poetry has always been my most favourite way in which to express feelings, thoughts, hopes and fears, and humour. It requires discipline and yet provides a wonderful freedom.

I would like to thank all the judges for being a part of this competition – with special gratitude to Pam Ayres and Brian Patten for agreeing to judge the two eldest categories. To have such eminent poets with us is truly inspiring.

I know I can speak for the other judges when I say that choosing 'winners' and 'highly commended' was a challenging task. Softened a little by the fact that many who were not selected have their poems published in this book.

And I must not forget the illustrators who have enhanced, in their individual ways, the words on the page.

How fortunate we are that a new generation of poets is emerging. The talent of many of them will, I am sure, blossom and grow. I only hope they never lose their ability to see the world and its creatures with an unbiased mind and clear eye and an open heart so they,

in turn, will inspire those young poets yet to be
discovered.

Virginia McKenna OBE
Founder and Trustee
Born Free Foundation

Year 3

Poems judged by Virginia McKenna OBE

Photograph © Maria Slough

Following a successful career as an actress, Virginia McKenna started Zoo Check in 1984 with her late husband, Bill Travers, and her eldest son, Will. This was after the premature death of Pole Pole, an elephant they had come to know during the filming of *An Elephant Called Slowly*, who was later gifted to London Zoo by the Kenyan Government. Zoo Check later became the registered charity Born Free Foundation. Whilst Virginia still finds time to work occasionally as an actress, her leading role now is within the conservation and animal welfare movement.

Virginia has also authored, co-authored and co-edited numerous books as well as travelling extensively over the years. Virginia also speaks at numerous events, supports various other charitable organisations and is patron to many others. In celebration of the charity's 30th birthday, and as a lover and writer of poetry herself, (her new poetry book *Tonight the Moon is Red* was published in October this year) Virginia was asked to judge the youngest of the age groups in this competition and what a difficult task it proved!

This is what Virginia had to say:

The winner and runners up write in very different ways and the poems are in stark contrast – but *Ethan's Acrostic* is extraordinary for a Year 3 child. Not only does Ethan evoke the individual worlds of different animal species so succinctly and vividly, but by reading down the first letters of each line you know he really understands what lies at the heart of Born Free's philosophy.

The Leopard Seal vividly paints the survival skills needed by this sleek, swift sea mammal. All seems fine until – the sharp warning at the end is a wake-up call. Needed even by this most skilled of hunters and understood by a skilled young writer.

The imagination at play in *Shadow Ponies* is remarkable, so even though not really about animals of any kind it is an extraordinary piece of work.

And then I could not leave out the two highly commended poems. *I Want to be Free* is a perceptive piece of writing from an obviously very aware young girl. We understand now, more than ever, what it means for a highly intelligent animal to live in captivity, and Ocearna has perfectly caught the terrible reality of the dolphin's life and its dreams of where it yearns to be.

Black Rhinos sends us the wake-up call from the start. The line which enticed me in is: 'And they are blowing out the rhinos' candle'. And good to read about how some humans do care.

Year 3 Winning Poem

Ethan's Acrostic

Bears lolloping, hunting for food.
Orangutans swinging from branch to branch.
Rattlesnakes slithering silently at night.
Narwhals swimming in the ocean depths.

Frogs leaping through the undergrowth.
Rabbits hopping and hiding shyly.
Eagles soaring through the air.
Elephants stomping over the earth.

I think these beautiful creatures deserve to have a
    wonderful free life
Just like you and me.

Ethan Pettifer, *Boothville, Northamptonshire*

Joint Runners Up

The Leopard Seal

Gliding through the Antarctic Ocean,
Camouflaged fur darting in the murky depths.
Swift and deadly, soft and sleek,
Speeding through icy waters like a torpedo.
Your penguin prey feel your powerful jaws,
Sharp and piercing, they show no mercy.
Keeping the company of only a few,
You bask on icebergs under the wintery sun.
In your watery playground you are the king,
You are the Leopard Seal.
While you are hunting for your next meal,
Silent danger lurks beyond,
Beware of those who are hunting you down.

Louie Fidler, *Byfleet Village, Surrey*

Shadow Ponies

Caution!
Invisible to the human eye
SHADOW PONIES.
Ten shadows dance in the moon's full rays,
These shadows can be seen by human eyes but not the
    owners of the shadows.
The shadow ponies can only be seen on the days of the
    eclipse,
You might be one in a million to see a shadow pony.
Otherwise they become invisible again,
You can only hear them on the day of the eclipse
And if you listen carefully you might faintly hear their chants.
We are kind but scary.
We are always curious.
That's why we follow you and make your shadows.

Amélie Krestovnikoff, *Bristol*

19

Highly Commended

I Want to be Free

I want to be free
I want to dive off into the sea
I want to swim and be free.

I don't like my tiny pool swimming round and
Round performing the same display every day.
I don't want to eat the fish from the bucket,
Let me out to catch my own
Let me out to find my home.

The crowd wave goodbye at the end of my show
But I have nowhere new to go.
I miss my family, I miss my friends,
Will this misery ever end?

I have hatched a plan to escape from man!
I am going to swim as fast as I can
And jump up high into the clear blue sky
And I will flap my fins to try and fly up high
And clear that wall that imprisons us all.
Here I will be forever free as I sail over the wall into the
    clear blue sea.

Ocearna Peres, *Launceston, Cornwall*

Occarna Peres, *Launceston, Cornwall*

Black Rhinos

Black rhinos are in deep danger,
They all need to be protected by a ranger.
Bad men are poaching rhino horns,
They cut them off and put them in medicine bottles,
    and make dagger handles.
And they are blowing out the rhino's candle.

On the sandy plains of Mkomazi,
They can breed and be free.
With my godfather Fitz,
Who loves them to bits.

Let them be free,
And then we can have a nice cup of tea.

Our Africa needs to be protected,
Together as friends of the rhino.
Please be good,
And do the right thing.

Kora Williams, *Warnham, West Sussex*

Other Year 3 Poems and Drawings

I Love Killer Whales in the Sea

I love killer whales in the wild
It really makes me smile.
In the sea their families are happy
They are free from captivity.
It makes me sad when you capture them
It's very bad you are scaring them.
Sunburnt in the pool, this is not cool
They are bored and lonely and die early.
Save them please and set them free
Live happily ever after, full of laughter.

Calum Allen-Day, *Romford, Essex*

Calum Allen-Day,
Romford, Essex

Lions, Tigers and Other Animals Too

Lions, tigers and other animals too
Should never be sent to a circus or a zoo.
Lions, tigers and other animals too
Should be free to wander through the world like me and you.
Lions, tigers and other animals too
Should never be poached by anyone like me and you.

Ridley Bowden, *Christchurch, Dorset*

Stripes by Isobel Frost, *Southmoor, Oxfordshire*

Animals

I love animals just like you.
I love animals kangaroo.
I love animals so do you.
Leopards, cats, mouses too
I love animals just like you.

Charlotte Meadow Devlin, *Liphook, Hampshire*

A Happy Lion Family

Out in the Savannah, where it was very hot,
There lived a lonely lion, who liked to roam a lot.
One day on his travels, across the dusty plain,
Leon was searching for some water and hoping for
some rain.
He lay beneath a tree to take cover in the shade
But suddenly he heard a "ROAR', which made him
quite afraid.
He rose from where he lay and walked towards the sound
There he saw a lioness and a hyena fighting on the ground.
The hyena soon lay still and the lioness thought 'MEAT',
She had found herself some food and quickly began to eat.
But she wasn't going to share as this was her kill of the day,
And she hoped the onlooking lion would simply go away.
However, Leon wouldn't go and stayed there for a while,
He wasn't going anywhere, it just wasn't his style!
Soon they became friends and together walked the plains,
They hunted and shared their food and sheltered when
it rained.
It didn't seem long when up on higher ground,
Two furry bundles of joy were sleeping without making
a sound.
Leon and the lioness had made a family now, and together
they all lived happily,
The two cubs were new to the Savannah but most
special of all,
They had both been born free.

Olivia Cooper-Moncrieff, *Pembrokeshire, Wales*

Olivia Cooper-Moncrieff, *Pembrokeshire, Wales*

Scar the Lion

Here I am a deadly scary lion, stalking my prey.
It's a hard life being a lion, one second eating,
The next second drinking, I sometimes find it most confusing.

My mane is my best fancy-show for females.
I can get females with my golden mane shining.
My flashing jaws biting the flesh.
I am an agile ferocious and excited lion.

I move through the jungle like a creeping monster.
My jaws are like daggers and my claws
Are like sharp anchors pinning my prey down.

I have a sturdy body and lightning fast reactions.
I'm camouflaged in the growing wheat ready to pounce
With my earthquake roar
It can deafen all ears in the forest.

That's my life as a lion.

Harvey Ewart, *Ealing, West London*

The Lion

Here I am a deadly, scary lion stalking my prey.
My mane is like a sandy golden cloud.
When I roar like thunder the earth shakes.
I creep across the savannah.
As soon as I pounce on my prey my powerful claws
Dig into the scared, scared animal to murder it.
Some say I'm selfish but some say I'm clever.
Some animals in the jungle say I'm the prisoner of the jungle
But some say I'm the king.

Rosie Forbes, *Middlesex*

King of Fire

I will glide and leap through the magical air
As my long shaggy mane flows behind me.
My claws are as sharp as shining glass,
With my black, damp nose like a ball of liquorice.
I creep up and rage onto a vulnerable deer as it
    attempts to head home.
I am as harmful as a poisonous flower and when you
    lay a hand on me,
My body will give you a spark of horror.

Lola Harrison, *Hounslow, London*

Snow Leopards in the Wild

A Snow Leopard lives up high in the mountains,
And when the snow melts it's a bit like a fountain.
It likes to mess about,
And sniff with its snout!
A Snow Leopard hunts for prey,
So that they can stay
On the earth.

When the cubs come,
They like to stay with their mum!
Cubs are very cheeky,
Mum teaches them to be sneaky.
When it's bedtime,
Cubs go, "Whine, whine!"
Ready for another day of fun!
When the next day comes in sight,
Mum goes off to find a bite!
The cubs go, "Yum, yum!"
And then another cub (a friend) comes to see Mum
And asks, "Can I come and play?"

William Marr, *Burgess Hill, West Sussex*

The Lion

I rampaged through the jungle like a shooting star
    looking for food
With my dagger like teeth,
My bronze mane glinting in the sunlight.
I lurk in the shadows about to pounce on my weak prey.
My paws pushing down on the soft grass.
Suddenly I pounce on my struggling prey.
I look like a flaming statue.
My mane shining in the sun.
I howl a mighty roar shaking the ground like an earthquake.

Zack Taylor, *Richmond, London*

Leaping Lemurs

Leaping lemurs jump and twist
You never know they might just miss.
They love the trees and climb so high
Perhaps they wish that they could fly.
Their tails are like a wiggly worm
Climbing trees they twist and turn.
They use their tails as a crook
And hang off branches like a hook.
Eating nuts and lots of fruit
Thinking that they look so cute.
Their eyes are wide and dark and round,
Lemurs make a whooping sound.

Cameron Irvine, *Witley, Surrey*

King Cobra

It looks like an Egyptian King.
It sneaks on the back of its meat.
Its teeth are tougher than iron with venom
And even one little drop and you're dead.
It camouflages in the wheat.

Caleb Walker, *Braunstone Town, Leicestershire*

Lions...

A lion's mane is like a ring of flames.
When it hunts it looks like a golden ball
Walking like a quiet mouse to catch its prey.
Its claws climb up a tree like knives stuck into the tree
And it hunts like the wind and roars.
He's camouflaged like golden sand
And has teeth like daggers
And is as sturdy as 1000kg stuck to the floor
And the lion is strong as a bulldozer.

Tom Yost, *Kew, Surrey*

This Busy Tiger by Nicole Burke, *Cappawhite, Ireland*

Year 4

Poems judged by Debz Hobbs-Wyatt

Debz Hobbs-Wyatt works full time as a writer/editor and is the founder of Paws n Claws Publishing. She has a Masters in Creative Writing although her first degree is in Zoology, and she has a Masters in Ecology, so she is also a great animal lover! Debz has had over twenty short stories published in collections and been short-listed in a number of prestigious writing competitions including the Commonwealth Short Story Prize 2013. She was also nominated for the US Pushcart Prize in 2013 and won the inaugural Bath Short Story Award.

While No One Was Watching is her debut novel, an adult psychological thriller that was published last year by Parthian Books.

Debz loves to encourage children to write as she won her first writing competition with an animal story at the age of ten! She also runs workshops in schools, where she teaches children creative writing and is thrilled to be involved with this project!

This is what Debz had to say:

Wow! While I dabble in poetry from time to time, I was truly amazed to see what these young poets were producing. Not only do they all show wonderful fluidity and style in their writing, there is maturity I didn't expect. It's not easy constructing a great poem; it takes even the great poets many years of honing their craft – let alone producing something with an important message – as these children have done! I wanted them all to win! While I had to choose a winner and runner up and choose some to highly commend, my favourites did change. It is subjective and I'm sure you will feel the same! All worthy of inclusion in this special book.

That said, I chose *The Robin* as my stand-out favourite for several reasons. The language just seems to capture the essence of this enigmatic yet common British bird, I can see it, feel the movement of it and the colours Aliya creates so magically. This was always the winner for me. And a little bird we see all the time in the UK. Very special.

An Elephant's Prayer stood out amongst many worthy poems about elephants and poaching for the rhythm and the language, the message drummed home with the trampling of the elephant's feet. The message is strong and powerful and this one stayed with me.

I Love Animals I highly commended because of the rhythm and the simple honesty of the language. Lovely! *The Endangered Tiger* for the message, the imagery. Just great! *Haunting Hippo* – how mature and wonderful the language! Wow! And *The Seagull* because it was an unusual choice and seagulls get a bad rap though they are such clever birds.

Year 4 Winning Poem

The Robin

My little Robin's wintery view
He flies so fast
Through the silvery hue.

Silvery snowflakes
Tinkling too
Flying through the burning blue.

The red robin flies
Through the frosty skies
A torrent of windy snow
Winter's silvery glow.

A robin lands on a
Lonely lake
Just as the sun is about to break.

Aliya Hamdani, *London*

Runner Up

An Elephant's Prayer

Trampling through the jungle,
As careless as can be,
While out of sight the poachers,
Are closing in on me.

They want me for my majestic tusks,
Or so I have been told,
But what use is a tusk to man,
Except it can be sold.

And now I fear the end is near,
I hear their muffled feet,
I smell the air around me,
I feel the summer heat.

It may be too late for me soon,
But I will not die in vain,
For good men will surely win the battle
To save my children's reign.

Benjamin Reid, *Bookham, Surrey*

Highly Commended

I Love Animals

I love animals.

Crocodiles can crawl
Crocodiles can creep
Crocodiles can float
Crocodiles can sleep.

I love animals.

Monkeys have fun
Monkeys can swing
Monkeys can climb
Monkeys can cling.

I love animals.

Elephants are brave
Elephants can charge
Elephants are grey
Elephants are large.

I love animals.

Penguins can swim
Penguins can waddle
Penguins can slide
Penguins can toddle.

I love animals.

Cheetahs can run
Cheetahs can eat
Cheetahs have spots
Cheetahs eat meat.

I love animals.

Harvey Cook, *Bookham, Surrey*

The Endangered Tiger

I can't find a tiger in the forest,
I have been looking, honest.
He has black and yellow eyes,
That helps him see the skies,
Hunting for tasty meals to eat,
Killing for some fresh, juicy meat.
He has orange fur with big black stripes,
Scars on his shoulders to show his fights.
Squinting and closing his eyes, shows he is happy,
But he does not purr like an ordinary tabby.
He may be fierce with man his worst enemy they say,
If they continue to hunt him he may not be with us one day.
His fine quality fur fetches good money on the market,
And his meat may fill a prize Sunday basket.
It doesn't matter what you say,
Leave the tigers alone to play,
And let them live for another day.

Oscar Harman, *Dorking, Surrey*

Haunting Hippo

Pool water, dark brown and still,
No sign of movement until,
Ripples slowly start to appear,
I think I see a tiny ear.

Two eyes staring, small and round,
I wish I was still on solid ground,
I am not tricked by the eerie quiet,
This unpredictable beast will add me to its diet.

Weighing as much as a pick-up truck,
I think maybe I am out of luck,
His tusks are sharp and vast,
My life may not last.

I retreat as quickly as I can,
This bulky beast can swim faster than any man,
Slowly and silently it drops out of sight,
This experience gives me a terrible fright.

Cole Powell, *East Horsley, Surrey*

The Seagull

The seagull hovers over,
Waiting for you to look away,
When, SNATCH!
Who stole my cake today?

The seagull will eat anything,
But he is also someone else's lunch.
The sea eagle is on the watch,
Looking for something to munch.

The seagull is a clever bird,
Dropping clams onto the rocks.
It cracks them open,
Breaking their tight locks.

The seagull's cry
Makes our holiday complete
As it fills the sky
When it prepares to eat!

Max Watkinson, *Gomshall, Surrey*

Other Year 4 Poems and Drawings

Super Sharks

Super sharks:
Slowly searching the sea, the shark swims this way and that.
The shark eats many things, but it loves fat.
When it attacks it comes from beneath.
Preparing its razor sharp teeth.
Catching its prey off-guard
It hits very, very hard.
Their skin is made of denticles instead of scales.
Unlike fish and whales.
Although sharks kill us, we kill sharks more.
Sharks swim, they do not walk on the floor.
Some sharks are harmless especially the largest.
Wonder which one is the fastest?
There are lots of different sharks;
But none fly like larks.
Baby sharks are called pups;
Unlike humans they do not drink out of cups.
One of the reasons why they are such successful predators
Is because of their senses.
Sharks are free; they are not guarded by fences.

Warrick Agar, *West Clandon, Surrey*

The Indian Python

Beware the Indian python,
Slithering slyly through the night.
Hunting down his prey tonight,
Growing and growing in the light.
Solid muscle don't sleep tight.
If you live near be prepared for the night – and don't
    get the fright
Because at night
He does bite.

Amy Campbell, *Braunstone, Leicestershire*

Snow Leopard

I am a leopard. I live in snow,
My life is hard and full of sorrow.
I live in the mountains all alone,
My cave is littered with old goats' bones.
My fur is thick and covered in spots,
The hunters want it lots and lots.
They are going to catch me, they're tracking me down,
I've got to be stealthy, there are poachers around.

Edward Cox and Felix Wood, *Gomshall, Surrey*

Jaguar

Jaguars jumping
And
Growling, now
Up
And
Running.

Felix Dosmond, *Cobham, Surrey*

Animals of the Wild

Highly strung and playful,
Obedient nervous animal,
Rears up high when scared and excited.
Shiny coat, silky mane and tail as bright as a sparkling star
Elegant to watch and soft to touch.

I Hollidge, *Cranleigh Prep School, Surrey*

The Red Mist!

I poked my head out of the burrow,
My nose twitched left then right.
My head twisted right then left.
No big bad wolf in sight.

I scampered out of the burrow,
My brother and sister and I.
We frolicked about for a bit,
Nipping at leaves as we played.

I woke up early one morning,
To find my brother's eyes had become red.
The red mist had descended upon us,
We looked at each other in fear!

I raced through the warren,
Passing sisters, cousins and aunts.
Racing to find my mother,
To tell her the mist had arrived.

For the next few days this all happened,
My brother couldn't see anything at all.
My brother was sick,
As sick as a dying plant.

We ran past houses, buildings and fields,
Until we found a spot that was safe.
We ran away from the disease,
To leave my brother in peace.

Ben Hulford-Funnell, *East Horsley, Surrey*

Reindeer

Racing through the crystal white snow
Reindeer with:
Long antlers on the top of their small, brown heads;
    long, strong legs
Golden fur covering their bodies.
They work day and night, training to pull the sleigh on
    Christmas Eve
But all are envious of that famous one, you know who I
    mean,
That gets to pull the sleigh that special night.

Arjun Kang, *Guildford, Surrey*

Wild Times

As the sun came up the wild times began…

Wild cats were having a race,
The lion trotted along thinking he's ace,
The tiger beat her paw on the ground,
And the hyena made a cackling sound.

The apes were collecting bananas,
The monkey swung over a sea of piranhas,
The gorilla banged his chest and hopped down from his
    perch,
But the baboon walked past and carried on his search.

The crocodile clan were trying not to be seen,
The caiman camouflaged themselves amongst yellow
    and green,
The alligator smirked,
Whilst the crocodile lurked.

The mammals were having fun in the sun,
The orca was on the run,
The dolphin clicked as he tricked,
And above the waves the whale's tail flicked.

But as the sun went down silence returned.

Bayley Knights, *Edgware, Middlesex*

The Scorpion

The scorpion moves along the desert floor scurrying
Like the spider, its tail of poison is as sharp as
A lion's tooth and its poison is as deadly as a bite.
Its black scales of darkness that reflect the sun's light.

Kenneth Ma, *Glenfield, Leicestershire*

The Tiger

Tremendous claws have I,
When food is close,
I don't deny.
Indonesia is my home,
Though we are many,
I hunt alone.
Great at pouncing so they say,
With a final leap,
I catch my prey.
Even if they struggle and shriek,
My terrifying jaws will make them weak.
Rarely do I come back home,
Without some meat upon a bone.

Columbus Mais-Harding, *Dorking, Surrey*

Cheetah

Cheetah runs
His speed awesome
Eating Impala
Each one feeling his power
Tail stretched for balance
Africa is his
Home!

Rabecca Mufalali, *Tujatane School, Livingstone, Zambia*

Rabecca Mufalali,
Tujatane School, Livingstone, Zambia

Turtles

Turtles are reptiles,
They are cold blooded too,
They have a hard shell,
To protect what they do.
They have a special gland
And lay eggs in the sand.
Turtles are endangered, so do
All that you can,
To stop the attack,
That comes from man!

Jack O'Neill, *Cobham, Surrey*

50

Elephant

I was born in the wild,
I was born to be free,
With lots of other animals,
Who are just like me!
I grew up strong,
Protecting my herd,
But then one day,
Gunshots were heard.
I charged at the men,
I trampled the gun,
I feared for my life,
Whilst they had their fun!
I want to be here,
I have a right to be me,
Stop the poaching and gunfire,
And give me my right to be free.
Majestic and proud,
An elephant of might,
With no gun of my own,
I will one day lose the fight.

Sophie Rommel, *Timperley, Manchester*

Zebra

Zambia's pride
Eating grass
Black and white stripes
Running
About.

Vanessa Siagaba, *Tujatane School, Livingstone, Zambia*

Animals

Lions run the world
Toucans sight-see from birds eye views.
Hummingbirds hum their hearts out,
Frogs leap for their lives,
Elephants squirt water higher than the moon.
The Kingfisher bird dives into the water like an
    Olympic swimmer.
So we need our animals or the world will be nothing.

J Taylor, *Cranleigh Prep School, Surrey*

J Taylor, *Cranleigh Prep School, Surrey*

The Lion

Lovely silky mane, swishing in the gentle breeze
Inky red blood dripping as he walks
On your marks! Ready to pounce on its prey
Nice slow pace for creeping.

M Taylor, *Cranleigh Prep School, Surrey*

The Saola

Sharp long horns, white markings on its face
This Asian unicorn moves without a trace
Through wet, low forests which were once its home
This mysterious creature has no place to roam.
Snares and development threaten their life
Why do we cause such strife?
Shy, gentle creatures who mean no harm
The rarest of mammals with mysterious charm
They find themselves endangered by us
So to save them let's make a fuss.
Snares and development threaten their life
Why do we cause such strife?

George Williams, *Abinger Hammer, Surrey*

Year 5

Poems judged by Virginia McKenna OBE

This is what Virginia had to say...

Have you ever seen...? just had to be first. India-Amethyst's imagination and the way she whirls us along with her images and her humour is just wonderful. And, for me, her skill is that following the fun and frolicking path she has led us along, she quietly brings us into the real world. The world she likes best. Marvellous.

So very different are the two poems in joint second place, but somehow they connect because of the economy of language, simplicity of description. *A Tale of Two Elephants* by Sophie Casey starkly tells us the difference – for elephants – of a captive and a free life.

Dutch Warmblood by Mia Walker is about a horse. I believe a wild one but somehow it doesn't matter. It is about the freedom of an animal to be itself and the deep protective instincts of a mother for its young. These three winners have, in my view, great talent and I hope they will keep writing. And imagining.

My Highly Commended list is probably much too long! I did have seven but it was just so hard to leave any out! I'm afraid I had to, but all of them will be in this book.

Swinging Free! by Sami MacRae. This is about atmosphere. About an animal's life when man isn't around – stalking, hunting, killing. It is *'A Day in the Life of...'*. A real treat.

54

Cheating the Cheetah by Ben Rees: vivid, action-packed. I see it all. And humour too!

How does it feel to be an animal? – I really enjoyed this concept – intriguing, with the unexpected twist at the end.

Run Lion Run by Ella Waring – Good to read the lion's point of view. And perceptive too – man without his gun is nothing. The lion will always be king.

Year 5 Winning Poem

Have you ever seen...?

Have you ever seen...?
Have you ever seen...a bull do the Tango,
Throwing his partner to and fro?

Have you ever seen...an elephant read a magazine,
Laughing as they read?

Have you ever seen...a rabbit,
With the bad habit of picking its nose?!

Have you ever seen...a cat bouncing on a trampoline,
Waiting to scare a dog?

Have you ever seen...all this and more?
Well neither have I...so join me and my amazing
    imagination,
For massive, chaotic, thoughts of animals GALORE!
And maybe we'll see...a time when pigs have learnt to
    count to three,
Or adult giraffes are as small as me!
Or chickens with Mohicans playing hard rock,
Or a kangaroo playing the kazoo to a friend of his,
Who is a shrew.

Or maybe we won't,
For this is my imagination and real animals are better,
In real-life we could see:
A mighty pride of lions in the savannah,
Their shimmering golden fur transforming them into
    the flowing golden grass,
Or a tigress in the jungle,
Watching and waiting for the slightest movement,
Ready to strike upon her prey,
Or ducks playing in the muck of a murky pond.
I love animals you see,
And I think they love me,
So I like to spend my day,
Imagining how they live and how they play!

India-Amethyst Thakrar, *Lewes, East Sussex*

India-Amethyst Thakrar, *Lewes, East Sussex*

Joint Runners Up

A Tale of Two Elephants

Standing miserably, behind those bars,
Gazing helplessly at the stars.
Pacing round in such distress,
Why does the world have to be in this mess?

I was born to be wild and free,
Not condemned to this captivity.
If only the world would stop and care,
Why are they so unaware?

Running round, happy and free,
Vegetation, friends and family.
Giant trunks, flapping ears,
Healthy, strong and free from fears.

We are able to walk and roam,
The savannah is our natural home.
We as elephants never forget,
Losing us will be the world's biggest regret.

Sophie Casey, *Cheltenham, Gloucestershire*

Dutch Warmblood

Soft as silk, varnished as glass is,
Its mane sways side to side like a flag in the breeze.
As strong as metal bars but sometimes awfully gentle
    that you can see its muscles ripple.

It's so brave that it doesn't know the meaning of fear
And it leaps into battle like a locust,
When the horse is out of breath its snorting is like a
    dragon breathing hot steam.

She wraps her front leg round her struggling foal.
She has enough strength for the two.

Inspired by Job 39:19-25

Mia Walker, *Braunstone Town, Leicestershire*

Highly Commended

How does it feel to be an animal?

Sometimes I feel
Like an animal
Sometimes a lion or even a seal
It turns like a wheel.

Today I can fly
I am an eagle
And I could
Do something illegal.

Tomorrow it depends
Maybe a wild dog
Or maybe a hog
I will think on a log.

When my parents
Make me drink tea
I feel like I want to sting them
Like a bee.

When I win
I feel like a dolphin
And I dream
That I swim.

And I wonder
What will be
If an animal would want
To be like me.

Maria Kagan, *Lisbon, Portugal*

Swinging Free!

The light is dancing through the trees
Oh how it feels to be free!
The jungle is buzzing all around
With squawking, squeaking, humming sounds.

As I am swinging with my tail
I try to reach a branch, but fail
Catching myself without a fault
I whoop with joy and somersault.

Parrots squawk, jaguars growl,
Hummingbirds hum and the monkeys howl
As the sun slowly walks away –
There it comes, the close of day.

I climb up high into a tree
I am as happy as can be.
Evening breezes flutter through the air
I just sit on a branch, and stare…

Sami MacRae, *Lewes, East Sussex*

Sami MacRae, *Lewes, East Sussex*

61

Cheating the Cheetah

My home is the African plain
Speed is my middle name.
Black spots cover my back
My perfect nose helps me follow and track.

I sense a gazelle running fast
Afraid it will soon go past.
Will it be an easy prey?
Will I eat a meal today?

I sneak up in the tall grass
Out of hiding in a flash.
0-60, I start to drool
It's time to kill, fast food is cool!

I jump up and bite its neck
And rake my claws across its back.
I wrestle it to the ground
And squeeze 'til it makes no sound.

I taste blood in my mouth
Lick my teeth from north to south.
I relish the flesh on my tongue
It feels good, but I'm not strong.

I start to yawn, retract my claws
Feels like it's time to pause.
My eyelids are now drooping
0-1 seconds and I'm sleeping.

I hear a laugh and dream it's me,
But it's a hyena stealing my tea.
You might say it's the steal of the day
But I call it a fast food take-away!

Ben Rees, *Bingley, West Yorkshire*

Ben Rees, *Bingley, West Yorkshire*

Run Lion Run

Whenever I sleep
Whenever I leap
Whenever I eat, the cold raw meat.
Whenever I roar
There's always a hunter beside me, I'm sure.

Whenever he shoots,
I run like the wind.
Whenever he shouts,
He may feel doubt.
For all the weapons he brings,
"Ha!" I'm still king!!!

"But man I'm here, standing here
If you listen then you will be clear
That the king of all animals
Has no FEAR!"

Ella Waring, *Barnes, London*

Other Year 5 Poems and Drawings

The Ginger Cat

He is as gingery as a ginger biscuit.
He is sharper than a knife.
He is as quick as a piece of lightning.
His tail swishes with the wind.
His eyes are like a snake.
His whiskers whistle with the wind.
His hearing is as good as an elephant.
He is a hero in the movies.
He is as vicious as a shark.
He's sneaky, he is silent,
He's unknown.
He is a pussycat?

Eliyah Austin, *Blaby, Leicestershire*

Animal Homes

There are animals on land,
There are animals in sea,
There are animals everywhere,
Living with me!
There are animals in trees,
There are animals next door,
There are animals near you,
Just go and explore!

Anya Constantinescu, *Alveston, Bristol*

The Blue Dragonfly

Burning blue eyes as bright as the sun,
Spiralling and twirling, having lots of fun.
Soaring through the skies here I go!
"I'm that beautiful dragonfly you know."
Elegantly I glide through the air,
As my shining cloak wide wings wave goodbye to the
    deep, dark lair
Brown as mud I was and feared of too,
But now I'm a majestic beauty just like you.
You may not have thought it but I did have a friend,
But sometimes good things come to an end.
That's it then here I go,
I'm a dragonfly and that's all you need to know.

Brooke Leah Daniels, *Sidcup, Kent*

Brooke Leah Daniels, *Sidcup, Kent*

Animal Frenzy

If it weren't for you Born Free,
What would happen to me?
I could be in a zoo,
Not far from you,
Or at a poacher's spot,
Waiting to be shot.
Monkeys in cages,
There for ages,
Mistreated and sad,
How come people are so bad?
In a water park,
Where sea lions are forced to bark,
When they would rather be back in the sea,
Where they are free.
Lions and tigers,
Monkeys and cheetahs,
Giraffes and pandas,
Koalas and zebras.
Leopards and panthers,
Gorillas and lemurs,
Now saved and free,
We all live happily.

Albane Fery, *Wimbledon, London*

What am I?

I move as fast as an arrow from a bow
So my prey never knows who I am.

I climb as well as a spotted gecko
My brother is the jaguar, my cousin is the leopard.

I live upon the savannah
My prey are the leaping gazelles of the grassland.

Now the final question
With all this information
Answer this...
What am I?

A cheetah.

Bethany Harrison, *South Wigston, Leicestershire*

The Cat and the Mouse

The Cat and the Mouse went to space,
On a supersonic swarm of bees,
They took a hat and a baseball bat,
Wrapped up in a slice of cheese.

The Cat looked down at the moon below and cuddled
    up to the Mouse,
"O Mouse my darling! O darling Mouse,
What a charming Mouse you are, you are
What a charming Mouse you are."

The Mouse whispered to the Cat, "Let's go for a walk.
    Too long we have sat."
"Oh Mouse, how sweet your words come through,
We shall go for a walk so we can talk,
But what shall we do for some shoes?"

They walked on their hands across sea and sands
Through jungles and deserts
Till they found the land where the Leprechaun lives
And there on his foot a pair of shoes stood!

Molly Jones, *Milton-Under-Wychwood, Oxfordshire*

Endangered Animals

All endangered animals, listen to me,
Now, listen up closely.
You've got to be brave,
You've got to be strong,
You've got to stop poachers from shooting along.
So listen up animals,
I may have a plan,
But only if you be
As fierce as you can.
All you little youngsters,
You stay at home.
Your parents are scared
But they're not alone.
So all of you out there,
Please, please help,
Even you fish
That live in the kelp.

Lauren King, *Cropwell Bishop, Nottinghamshire*

Duck

Duck. What does it need?
It needs help, and safety, from others.
As in the forest, the route ahead,
It's much much worse than your nice warm bed.

Duck. What could it do?
Too simple minded to be true.
What defence does it have against,
Against the cunning snake.

Duck. Who created this one?
The simple minded and the dumb?

Duck. When has this creature faced the terror?
Or has it faced it yet?
If it did, it would be dead.
Tigers, snakes and spiders too,
What would this hopeless creature do?

Duck. What does it need?
It needs help, and safety, from others.
As in the forest, the route ahead,
It's much much worse than your nice warm bed.

Isaac Samuel Silverov, *London*

Year 6

Poems judged by Lauren St John

Lauren St John is a highly successful and acclaimed author; she is also an ambassador for the Born Free Foundation.

She is the author of several books on sports and music, including *Hardcore Troubadour: The Life & Near Death of Steve Earle*; and the multi award-winning children's series, *The White Giraffe, Dolphin Song, The Last Leopard* and *The Elephant's Tale. Dead Man's Cove*, the first in her mystery series featuring eleven-year-old detective, Laura Marlin, who lives in St Ives, Cornwall, won the 2011 Blue Peter Book of the Year Award and was shortlisted for Children's Book of the Year at the Galaxy National Book Awards. Her first adult novel, *The Obituary Writer*, was published by Orion in June 2013. Her new horse book, *The Glory*, will be published by Orion in 2015.

This is what Lauren had to say:

What a difficult job it was to choose from such talent! I'd have to say I was torn but in the end, after much deliberation, I chose as my winner, *A Glint of an Eye* by

Sophien Amrani for its evocative language. Sophien paints a vivid picture of the beauty and wonder of nature. A worthy winner.

A close runner up, interestingly, happens to be our winner's brother Adam Amrani with *The Phantom of Night*. They do the hardest and best things in all writing, which is to transport the reader and make them feel. A wonderful job!

I also feel I had to highly commend Miya McFarlane's *To Win a Fight*. She takes the reader to the heart of the bullring and shows it for the evil that it is. While she's chosen to write about bulls, the issues and emotions she explores could be applied to any situation where animals are captive or abused.

Year 6 Winning Poem

A Glint of an Eye

The silent claw print,
The beating wing,
The white mystery,
The snowy wonder.

A dark rim of black around the eye,
Tells a story worth a lifetime,
Laced with white feathers,
It flaps across the barren waste land.

The thick plumage and feathered talons,
Keep it warm and alive,
A sharp glint of a cunning eye
Frightens the toughest souls.

When the sky is lit up by the sun,
And the snow has started to melt,
The pale wise wizard searches across the land
To protect its only home.

The ashen white feathers,
Break the contrast of its heavy black beak,
As it cushions its delicate face,
Against its hollow crest.

The white quill against the tundra's soft snow,
Reveals only the glimpse of a yellow eye,
This powerful and elegant creature,
Thrives through the snowy forest.

The silent formidable hunter,
 Waits for the right time to dive,
The soundless wing,
Helps to pounce on prey in stealth.

Sophien Amrani, *Harrow, Middlesex*

Sophien Amrani, *Harrow, Middlesex*

75

Runner Up

The Phantom of Night

The sky wears its jumper of gloom as the bat
With droopy eyes hangs from a decrepit branch,
Its charcoal black skin camouflaging in the dark
Like the solemn cloud before the dusk.

The debauched bat takes off in a storm of wings
Its small body fluttering away into the dim twilight sky,
The winter night is incandescent with starlight,
As the canvas of the moon hangs like a luminous pearl
    from paradise.

Voracious, the bat's flattened spade shaped nose
Soaks up the animal aroma on the night's wind,
The impenetrable and disorientating blackness
Forces the bat to alter its enchanted headlights of crimson.

As it is led by its ribbon of light,
It dives into a mouth of obscurity,
It senses a glimpse of gold
Just before it plunges down onto a destitute moth.

Adam Amrani, *Harrow, Middlesex*

Editor's Note: we were amazed when we saw that brothers took the first and runners-up spot in this category! Purely coincidence and it just goes to show what a talented family this is!

Adam Amrani, *Harrow, Middlesex*

Highly Commended

To Win a Fight

To win a fight, you must stand your ground.
So when the fighters come, strike back, hard.
The bull stood with his herd, and snorted.
Before him was a tall man, with rope and a syringe in hand.
He bared a snarl as the bull went docile.
And was pulled away.

To win a fight, you must not show fear.
So when the fighters come, do not crumple.
The men in black entered the barn all holding a bat.
Drugged and in pain,
The bull was hit again and again
Snorting and bellowing its innocent heart out.
His eyes sting and his sight recedes.

To win a fight, you must be strong, and be brave.
So when the fighters come, do not let your courage cave.
Hauled into a pitch black cell, the distressed bull is
      beaten once more.
A terrified snort escapes him as he crashes down to the
      floor.
His limbs feel dead, and from his head
Flows a dark river of red.

To win a fight, you must keep your head high.
So when the fighters come, strike back, don't crumple,
be brave, and don't give in.
In comes the fighter, but he wears no black
From his leather riding boots to his cowboy hat.
A flag of red, like a danger banner, tied to his sturdy
    dark belt.
The bull didn't move, just gave a pained grunt... Well,
    pain was all he felt.
His horns were uneven, his legs and back were weak.
Yet he stood up and swayed out the door,
His patience about to leak.
The fighters were there, some with horses, tensed up to fight,
Such an intimidating sight.

To have a fight, the conditions must be fair, the fighters
    must be fair, the FIGHT must be fair.

The bull? It never stood a chance.

Miya McFarlane, *Hemel Hempstead, Hertfordshire*

79

Other Year 6 Poems and Drawings

Evermore

Elegant
It spreads those long white wings
As soft as eiderdown
And glides through the air
The snow around it like white confetti
Falling from the sky.

Swimming
Through a crystal clear lake
A queen to the nature
Surrounding it.

Hidden away
Amongst the reeds
There lies a nest
Filled with new life.

Standing
Under the spotlight of the moon
A white angel
Wings spread wide
Guards over
A basket filled with love.

As blossom floats down
From the trees
A grey and white parade
Glides down the lake
Majestic
Together
For evermore.

Maryam Alatmane, *Small Heath, Birmingham*

What would it be like?

What would it be like to be a sheep?
To be able to majestically leap
Or to be a cow
But I wonder how?
To be a proud horse;
But I won't forget of course.
The power of a bird
To call, and be heard
Or to be a dog with fur.
What would it be like
To be a creature?
To be full of peace and love,
I'd have to be a dove
Or a bat flying over the eclipse
In the middle of an alpaca-lypse
Or to be a rat.
What would people think of that?
Maybe a cat beginning to purr
What would it be like
To be a creature?
All my fears would be swept aside
If I was part of a lion pride.
Imagine being a lizard
Getting caught in a strong blizzard
Or a magnificent peacock
Part of a colourful flock.
Maybe a cunning snake
Living by a calm lake
But that is not all
What would it be like to be mythical?

Juliet Elizabeth Priddey Allarton, *Halesowen, West Midlands*

Born Wild and Free

Free is like
The horse
Who does so much to please
Born wild and free.

Free is like
The lion
King of you and me
Born wild and free.

Free is like
The bird
Who flies so gracefully
Born wild and free.

Free is like
The elephant
Who pays no fee
To be born wild and free.

Free is like
The deer
Who is so glee
To be born wild and free.

Free is like
The fish
Who lives in the sea
Born wild and free.

Free is like
The animals
Air, land and sea
Born wild and free.

Zeta Ashmore, *Carlow, Ireland*

The Arctic Fox

The fox's fur is thick and white
When the winter sun is low but bright,
On this dark and gloomy night
He ducks and dives like a kite.

When the summer months come into sight
The fox's fur is brown and light.
It hunts and scavenges for its prey
And fills its belly both night and day.

The cubs and mother love to play,
They roll around and fight all day,
But when the bear comes into sight
The little foxes curl up so tight.

James Burke, *Cappawhite, Ireland*

Forest Symphony

The stealthy vixen, sneaks from her den as the last light
   of dusk fades.
The clumsy badger, crashes through bushes, making the
   first noise of the night.
A family of mice, cautiously edge from their hole,
   squeak, and go off to forage.
The owl's eyes slowly open and he hoots loudly, the
   symphony begins.

A bat, quickly shoots through the crisp night air,
   performing his acrobatics with pride.
The hedgehog snorts and snuffles, scuttling through the
   leaves.
A flying squirrel yells as he jumps from his tree and
   glides to the ground with ease.
The wild-cat struts through the wood, yowling, the
   symphony reaches crescendo.

The irritated wolf, pads from his cave, looks to the sky
   and howls, the signal for the symphony's end
All animals hear the keening note, the last sound of the
   night, they hurry back to den and burrow
Afraid to disobey the call, all the forest will sleep once
   more, until the next night's music.

Seren Grant, *Ruislip, Middlesex*

Seren Grant, *Ruislip, Middlesex*

The Beauty of the Tiger

A creature of beauty.
Creeping through the forest,
Ears pricked. Nose twitching.
Trotting briskly.

Stripy orange fire-fur,
Ruffled by the wind.
Wavy, like an ocean of silk.
Softly rippling.

Her eyes are emeralds,
As bright as stars.
They glisten and sparkle
With hope.

She stops, dead in her tracks.
Her heart beats faster.
Transfixed
Frozen in time.

She spies the hunters
And she knows
The Beauty of the Tiger
Will be gone tomorrow.

Niamh Irvine, *Wendover, Buckinghamshire*

Wild and Free

I want to be a tiger
Living wild and free
Not in a metal cage
In captivity.

I want to be an elephant
Living wild and free
Strolling around Africa
With my family.

I want to be an elephant
Roaming wild and free
Without scary poachers
Stealing my ivory.

I want to be a giraffe
Living wild and free
Growing tall and eating leaves
From the tallest tree.

I want to be a hippo
Living wild and free
Wallowing in the water
Happy as can be.

I want to be a chimpanzee
Living wild and free
Playing in the forest
And swing from tree to tree.

I want to be a lion
Living wild and free
Sleeping in the sunshine
Underneath a tree.

But I'm not an animal
I am only me
But we can help to put things right
With the help of Born Free.

Sienna Kelly-Todd, *Acton, London*

Cool Cockatoo

The cockatoo spread its gleaming, glossy wings.
Sparkly, beaded, silver strands,
Covered frisky feathers.
A gem fluttering iridescently in the sunshine.

The golden, gelled Mohican,
Flung back by the howling wind.
A model on the catwalk,
Strutting majestically on the silky sand.

It belts out a screechy song,
A squawking, raucous sound.
A cheeky child in the classroom,
Constantly demanding everyone's attention.

The occasional visitor passes by,
Extending crunchy cream crackers.
He and his friends line up as straight as a pin,
Pouncing on the lavish offering.

Razor sharp eyes,
Slicing through the dappled light.
It gazes at the serene sunset,
a tantalizing blend of earth, fire and water.

Rohan Kothari, *Watford, Hertfordshire*

The King of the Savannah

The long golden mane,
Glistens in the sun like fire,
The amber honey eyes,
Glint with hunger,

The lion prowls around the trees,
Watching every move of the deer,
Poised on its hunches,
Muscles tense and ready,

Majestic trees shiver in fear,
Timid creatures retreat back to their dens,
The lion's prey, alert, sensing danger,
Becomes rooted to the spot,

Heart pounding, eyes darting,
Unsure of what to do next,
Overhead, the birds start to screech,
As the ferocious beast leaps from the undergrowth,

Gripping, grasping and grappling,
Tearing meaty flesh from the limbs,
But, unknown to the lion, danger is lurking,
The greedy farmers want more land,

Bang, bang, bang, bang,
The sound that farmers are present,
The lion takes its last gulp of air,
The king of the Savannah is now dead.

Aman Mavani, *Northwood, Middlesex*

Aman Mavani, *Northwood, Middlesex*

Prey or Preyed

The wind was blowing with a roar,
Trying harder against it I did soar.
Made stronger and stronger by the sea and tide,
Making it more difficult for me to glide.

I clasped a branch and hunched my back,
The wind blew my feathers and then there was a Crack!
I quivered, quaked and a shiver went down my spine,
The sudden sound startled me off the pine.

I whizzed, zoomed and flew like a dart,
Swirling, curling making patterns of art.
Spinning around without even a flap,
Flying here and there without a navigation map.

Remembering my babies I needed to feed,
Spotting a prey, I dived down gathering speed.
The ground was in sight but-Bang, Boom, Crash, Smack!
Went something beside me and everything went black.

Vivek Nair, *Northwood, Middlesex*

Polar Bears

His skin was as soft as silk,
Claws as sharp as knives,
Fur as white as snow,
Nose black like soot.
The waking sun shone on his beautiful face.
The endangered creature was awake, yet
He was ravenous,
He got up as slow as a sloth.
Now he galloped up to the ice cold water,
And slid like a penguin into the arctic water.
His nose twitched,
He could smell his precious prey,
Suddenly out of nowhere he saw his solitary seal,
A huge seal.
He grabbed it in his massive paws,
Dragged it to shore
And gobbled it up in seconds.
He slowly wandered back to his enormous den.
He lay down as still as a statue,
Looked up at the diamond stars,
And dreamed about catching the seal all over again.

A Neve, *Cranleigh Prep School, Surrey*

Unite Children of the World – A Rhino's Plea

Is it because I am sluggish and bulky?
Is it because I am very shy?
Is it because I eat grass and plants?
Is it because I look old and wrinkly?
Is because I appear to have short stumped feet?
Is it because I have a small and large horn extended
     from my head, that you no longer care for me?
Remember I play a special part in nature's balance.
I make burrows in the sand and create places for my
     small friends to find food and grow.
My friend the ox pecker rests and searches for food on me.
Please, please help me…
There are not many of me left now.
Unite Children of the World, Unite.
Surely people listen to your calls.
You can make a difference in my fate as YOU are the
     future generation
This may be my last words to you
Shout, scream, write and speak to people that care
I don't know if I will be here tomorrow so please make
     the world hear my plea and last words
I am and will always be your very special friend.
Mr Rhino

Aaminah Patel, *Gauteng, South Africa*

Elephant Rampage

An elephant charged, shaking the ground,
Trumpet of a war cry pierced the silence,
A two tonned tank, it stampeded,
Destroying everything in its path.
People screamed in terror as he,
Stormed through the stone wall,
Spear like tusks tossed carts into houses,
Whilst villagers ran for dear life.
A helpless cow that stood in his way,
Was hurled high into the air,
Without warning a loud bang sounded.
Paralyzed, the mighty beast fell aground.

Tej Shah, *Hatch End, Middlesex*

Wolf by Casper Varoujian, *Bisley, Surrey*

Year 7

Poems judged by Richard Bonfield

Photograph
©Anna-Louise Pickering

Richard Bonfield is a poet of high acclaim and is the Poet in Residence for the Born Free Foundation. As a child he sleep-walked and dreamed that he saw pumas on the end of his bed and tigers leaping up the stairs.

Richard knew that he wanted to be a writer from the age of twelve but it was reading, at the tender age of fourteen, the poem *The Wind* by Ted Hughes that convinced him that he wanted to be a poet some day.

However, it wasn't until he turned thirty that he finally wrote his first poem, *First Fire*. Since then he has had over 350 poems published in over thirty magazines countrywide, and has self-published five collections of poetry, commencing with *A Bestiary: An Animal Alphabet*, which was included in the Books of the Year in the *Independent on Sunday* by Elspeth Barker in 1993.

Richard has also won many prizes for his work, and his poem *Zooplankton* was a winner in the BBC Wildlife Magazine Poet of the Year competition. But he says his most prized possession is the letter he received from Virginia McKenna that eventually led to his appointment as Born Free's Poet in Residence.

He is a great believer that we have all been given different gifts and that no one is any better than anyone else! Which is why having to choose a favourite from the year 7 poems was no mean feat.

This is what Richard had to say:

The poems in the eleven to twelve-year-old age group presented me with a wide range of styles, but the poems that really moved me were those where the child's imagination was unfettered and they were allowed to utilize their unique poetic voice.

I chose as my winner *Wilderness is Calling* by Francesca Muggli, because this poem addresses many of the issues that occupy Born Free on a daily basis. Wilderness is our true spiritual home, and without wilderness/wildness we will all feel impoverished and alone. The poet is actively engaged with a number of issues: the cruelty involved in taking creatures out of their natural environments for human delectation, and the processing of animals to satisfy human vanity. It is a poem about the inherent beauty/worth of creatures in and of themselves and is a very worthy winner.

My runner up is *The Snow Leopard* by Abigail Byrne, because of the haunting imagery that kept drawing me back to it. The poem has a Zen like clarity to it and a powerful sense of a mother's love, plus the necessity of survival at all costs in a world where humanity literally calls the shots.

Highly commended poems include *Lion-Warthog* by B Fewings, a poem I loved for its alliteration and its attention to detail e.g. 'The warthog's tail suddenly stood to attention', and for its arresting imagery such as the lion's heart-shaped nose and the lions mane frizzing like a Mexican wave. Wow! A short poem – but a poem shot through with humour and poetic awareness.

In K Wili's *Elephants*, the onomatopoeic 'thud, thud thud' is also exciting and immediate. I love the way she conjures up the image of the elephant with a few deft strokes of her poetic brush, and I was startled by the ending, which is as unexpected as it is unnerving.

Animals by Esmé Pathare is a wonderfully exuberant and joyful poem with some lovely imagery powered by a strong sense of rhythm and rhyme.

Alone by Jasmine Hooke is a lovely freewheeling empathic piece of writing as she attempts to put herself in the place of all those captive animals. A deceptively simple but profound piece of work.

Year 7 Winning Poem

Wilderness is Calling

Can you imagine a barren savannah, without a lion's cry?
Or the chopped rainforests, where all the trees have died?
Echoing woodlands, brutally split in two,
Now I can't imagine that, neither should you!

Pure, pearly ivory, belongs as elephant's tusks,
Not as elaborate carvings, described as 'pretty' husks.
Shimmering orange and black stripes, golden spotted fur,
Regal manes and feathers, cubs beginning to stir,
A blood-red sunset, tainted by twisted lies,
Too many empty promises, too many stolen lives,
Carried off to a zoo, or turned into a dress,
Tortured by ringmasters, what has caused this mess?
We're too busy preserving our own selfish needs,
Wilderness is calling, please take heed.

This plagues even the melting icy north,
Polar bears cruelly being brought forth,
Shipped away from their native homeland,
From icy glaciers to alien hot sand,
Hastily dumped under tight lock and key,
Fake snow shelters, rotting fish to feed,
Majestic whales, ripped to vile steak,
Ecosystems ruined, an awful mistake,
Snatched seal skin, human sin,
Throwing wilderness into a bin.

Is there light at the end of the tunnel?
Few sparks of hope, filtered through a funnel?
I believe, as one, we can reduce the need,
Wilderness is calling, please take heed!

Francesca Muggli, *Sintra, Portugal*

Runner Up

The Snow Leopard

Icy blue eyes,
Full of knowledge,
A glimpse of a different world,
A world where life and death are decided in a split second.

The misty oceans of suffering,
A snapshot of a mourning mother's pain,
She lost her cubs,
Their tiny lives taken
By a single golden bullet,
For poacher's sport.

The big cat prowls,
Her senses sharpened,
Her great busy tail, twitches, warning her prey,
She strikes, tearing at the raw flesh.
She must eat quickly, or she will join her cubs,
She will be killed, just like they were,
By a single golden bullet.

The ghost cat, curled up in a corner,
The last of her kind.
Never again shall we see her in the snow, and marvel at
her beauty.
Our children will ask, "What is that?" when they visit
the museum.
So now she is gone,
Her reign of wonder is over,
The moon cries out in anguish and the stars sing hymns
of sorrow,
For the mysterious cat of ice and snow is no more.

Abigail Byrne, *Fetcham, Surrey*

Highly Commended

Lion-Warthog

As the whistling wind whizzed vigorously past the warthog,
The lion's bloodshot eyes glared at him,
Craving his blood.
The warthog's tail suddenly stood to attention,
As his trepidation warned him that
He had been scouted by his predator.
The lion's lethal claws grasped the ground menacingly
As he lacerated the grass.
He pounced forward ferociously
To petrify his concerned prey.
His heart-shaped nose sniffed intensely
At the approach of his dinner.
As he charged forward a stampede of warthogs fled immediately
While his free-flowing mane frizzled
Like a Mexican wave.
The lion was left ravenous.

B Fewings, *Cranleigh Prep School, Surrey*

Alone

Have you ever known what it feels like to be alone?
You could be in a big crowd, and you're scared and
    make no sound.
You might be in paradise, but still miss your pet mice.
You might be at a party but later still need your big
    brother Artie.
You might be having chocolates, sweets and cakes
But later still miss how your mother bakes.
You could be at a sleepover and have lots of fun
But when it comes to sleep you miss your dad and mum.
Now have any of these things happened to you?
Yes?
Well that's how it feels to be on display at the zoo.

Jasmine Hooke, *Avening, Gloucestershire*

Animals

Animals are like jewels to a necklace,
Like nests hanging in a tree.
Like shells on a ragged and stormy beach,
They are special, like you and me.

To be a lover of these jewels,
Is like loving your mum and dad.
You care for them more than you care for yourself,
And you think they are totally fab.

They shouldn't be used for experiments,
They deserve to run wild and free.
For animals do good to planet Earth,
From rhinos to a bumble bee.

Animals are fun as well as cute,
Just think of playing with a kitten!
As a crazy and caring animal lover,
My feelings just can't be written!

Animals, oh animals,
You're as precious as gold.
You must be kept safe,
The world must be told!

Animals, oh animals,
You're as cool as TV.
No harm will be done to you,
I promise, you're free.

Esmé Pathare, *Dubai, United Arab Emirates*

Elephants

Thud, thud, thud
Earth shudders violently beneath me,
My colossal body wades through flowing streams
All sense of joy devoured by silence.

Coarse skin desperately clings to my vast structure,
My elongated funnel swoops elegantly,
Ears leisurely swing,
Right to left, up and down

Stop!
I stand in terror.
Straight ahead,
Shrieks of bewildering fear.

K Wili, *Cranleigh Prep School, Surrey*

Other Year 7 Poems and Drawings

Lions Roar

Silk fur shining in the African sun,
Lean muscles rippling with a spring in every stride,
Large head held high above the swishing grass,
Eyes like embers from a fire searching the silent horizon,
Enormous paws padding against the parched dry ground,
Silent in every step.
The prey standing vulnerable in the grass,
Not aware of the king of cats standing there staring,
Watching,
Waiting.
Within a heartbeat the prey is running for its life,
The lion bounding along effortlessly,
Gracefully,
Claws like daggers drag the prey down,
Teeth like icicles sink into the tender flesh,
The huge body of muscle flops happily onto the ground,
Prey limp in its iron jaws,
Suddenly a roar rips through the air,
The king howls in victory.

J Davis, *Cranleigh Prep School, Surrey*

In the Jungle by Kaela Aalto,
North Reading, Massachusetts, US

The Wild

As the spear of the night pierces its helpless victim,
The sun bleeds its blood,
The amber light blankets the sky,
And the sunset has come.

Whilst down beneath this moving spectacle,
On the barren plains of the void,
The African king stands tall,
The rhino stand proud.

The great black horn punctures the air,
It wears a heroic mask of defiance,
And it batters the jackal pests away,
The rhino cannot be thwarted.

Yet beneath the rhino's immense bulk,
Where muscle dominates the sun,
Another predator hunts,
The gecko is on the prowl.

The gecko's beady eclipse black eyes look onto its prey,
Slowly it propels itself forward like a clock-work toy,
Its skin sifts through the sand like a mirage,
Its plump tail curls in anticipation
And the gecko pounces.

Heavy boned jaws clamp down on the locust,
The gecko squeezes out the life
And slowly it engulfs the mutilated corpse,
A sickly yellow liquid seeps out of the locust's bulging eyes.

And as the jackals flee
As the locust dies
As the gecko eats
The sun goes down,
And another day passes in the wild.

C Hayley, *Cranleigh Prep School, Surrey*

Africa

At the dawn of my life, the sun arose from the horizon
   as silent as night.
It was calm and peaceful.
The sound of wildlife thriving filled my ears with a song
   of beauty.
I was as happy as could be.
I simply would watch the world pass me by and know I
   was safe.

Years later, at the eventide of my life, I walked across
   the horizon
With fear in my eyes and an anxious and uneasy step.
I think I must not make a sound.
There is no sound just a deadly silence.
I check the trees. Is there anyone there? No? Good.
Next tree. Am I safe? Wait! No-one's safe.
"Ahh," I sighed. "Will I ever be safe?

J Moore, *Cranleigh Prep School, Surrey*

The Tiger

The tiger moves through the open world
The tiger moves through the jungle
His jaws as powerful as a vice
The tiger moves through the stick thin trees
The tiger moves over the roots and leaves
The tiger's sharp eye sees the prey
The chase is on!

Leaping and bounding over the roots and leaves
Dodging through the stick thin trees
His vice like jaws ready to bite
Gaining, gaining
Biting, biting
The chase is gone!
The tiger moves through the jungle
The tiger moves through the open world
Disappears into the open world.

P Moor, *Cranleigh Prep School, Surrey*

The Music of the Jungle

The grass sways as the crickets sing their melody,
Like a natural orchestra playing day and night,
The lion prowls the area, its roar piercing through the
    peaceful lyric,
The canopy above is like a rainbow of dancing
    performers,
The lubricated, slimy snake slithers carefully through
    the dry, parched scrub,
Its scales rippling menacingly,
The life above the shrub chatters exuberantly as the
    monkeys cavort on high.

A O'Neil, *Cranleigh Prep School, Surrey*

Born Free

Fur like fluff and razor claws
Legs are stout and padded paws
Silently, creeping, listening.

Ears that prick and quick to hear
Tongues that lick from ear to ear
Silently, creeping, listening.

Tail like bristles on a brush
Mane like hair and flowing rush
Silently, creeping, listening.

Eyes like specs and twinkling stars
Teeth like knives and iron bars
Silently, creeping, listening.

Nuzzling and nestling in the flow
Of deep, deep water down below
Silently, drinking, listening.

J Porter, *Cranleigh Prep School, Surrey*

My Kingdom

I am part of this world.
I live in orange weeds and green bushes
Under my huge oak tree and I am very happy.
I close my brown eyes and dream,
Golden fur glistening in the sun,
Huge paws scraping the dirt, tail swatting flies.
This is the life, as I dream in the sun.
This is my kingdom, as the green leaves shimmer in the
golden light.

I sleep, I dream…

But trouble comes into my world,
I cannot feel the grass,
A net consumes me.
It is a woven hell, which I tear at with my teeth.
And now, thick bars through which I am laughed at.
It is dark now. Where is my green kingdom of wilderness?
The green has turned into a black kingdom forever and
always.

I sleep, I dream…

The only way back to my natural world is in my dreams.
I dream of my oak tree, my oak tree it was beautiful.
Bars of steel turn to vines of flowers
Everyone's cages turn to trees,
We all charge to the river flowers flowing close behind
And there, there is my oak tree.
I spring through golden grass,
Splash through the river, and roll into my kingdom
    once more.
I shake the water off my thick golden mane and out
    pours a rainbow with my loudest roar.

I sleep, I dream,
Am I home?

Daniel Waring, *Barnes, London*

Drawing by Cover Artist, Daniel Waring,
Barnes, London

The Sloth

The sloth's sleepy eyes unravel slowly revealing the
    misty forest.
The wonderful birds flutter above the canopy into the
    early morning sun.
His floppy arms wrap around the mossy trunk
    preparing to clamber down.
He sees some lush leaves, making his mouth grin cheekily.
He reaches the branch.
Chomp, chomp, chomp go his big white teeth as they
    chew the green leaves.
When he is done he notices a shadow far away.
Its jet black fur blends in with the shadows,
His razor sharp teeth glisten in the trees.
It is a leopard, a large black leopard.
The sloth turns back, scrambling towards its tree.
Right, left, right, left go his small stumps as they
    scramble up the trunk.
He turns around and spots the leopard, in the same place.
He gasps a sigh of relief.
And goes to sleep.

L Andrews, *Cranleigh Prep School, Surrey*

Lost Dreams

Stuck behind bars like a criminal,
Yet, I have committed no crime.
Paraded around like an exhibit,
For the crowds to cheer and laugh.
The stick comes down on my back,
And my feet are bound with chains
I don't live... I only exist.

I had a life, once upon a time,
Every day was heavenly,
Every day was blissful,
Every day was freedom,
Every day was happiness,
Every day was wishing, hoping, dreaming
But not now...

Life is putting on a show,
Life is being struck with a whip,
Life is pain and sorrow,
Life is cruelty and sadness.
If this is life,
I would rather die,
Die for my lost life,
My lost hope,
My lost dream.

Dulanya Cooray, *Mt. Lavinia, Sri Lanka*

Year 8

Poems judged by Brian Patten

Brian Patten came to notice in the 1960s as one of the Liverpool Poets, alongside Adrian Henri and Roger McGough. Their joint anthology, *The Mersey Sound* (1967), has been credited as the most significant anthology of the twentieth century for its success in bringing poetry to new audiences, and is now in Penguin Modern Classics. He has published over forty books and his poems are translated into many languages. They include *Collected Love Poems* (HarperCollins) and *Selected Poems* (Penguin Books). His books for children include *The Story Giant*, *Gargling With Jelly*, and *Juggling With Gerbils*. He is a fellow of the Royal Society of Literature.

It was a real honour for us that Brian agreed to be one of our esteemed judges and like the others was highly impressed by the quality of the entries for this older age group.

This is what Brian had to say:

I don't think there is ever such a thing as a 'best' poem, in the same way that there is no such a thing as a 'best' animal. Still, we can have personal favourites, and mine is *The Lion with a Heart* by Shara Burns. The poem describes the knowledge and emotion in a lion's eyes, along with its wonderful last line that gets a roar of approval from me! In the poem the poet shows a great empathy for the creature she is writing about. The poem makes you stop and think about the lion in a different way: why shouldn't the lion be a loving kitten – it was that very thing once upon a time.

What it Means to be Born Free by Morgan Joy Ashby is another wonderful poem, full of mystery. Often poems work best by leaving things out – by letting the reader do some of the work, and Morgan Joy Ashby has discovered this instinctively. This is a poem by a born poet.

We can't leave out comic verse! Good comic verse looks deceptively easy to write, but it's not. *My Friend Rhino* by Sinesipho Wali is both simple and inventive. Rhyming 'trusted' with 'rhinocerusted' makes for a perfect ending!

Year 8 Winning Poem

The Lion with a Heart

Every step of a lion's paws flood you with fear,
When they just want to know you, to ask why you're here.
The roar of a lion splits you apart,
Until you find that this lion, this lion has a heart.

You think he is going to mangle you, eat you all up,
But the truth is he's lonely, he needs cheering up.
For if you stare wistfully into a lion's eyes,
The knowledge and emotion will take you by surprise.

Dip your toes in the oasis and not water will you find,
But an aura of fantasy that ripples through the night.
Stare into the sky and not stars will you see,
But a million tiny fireflies dancing in the trees.

When you slowly and softly place your hand upon a lion's fur,
You feel loved, you feel free, like life is just a blur.
Yet this moment is so real, so true and so clear,
A lion is merely a loving kitten, trapped inside
    something that we all fear.

Shara Burns, *Harwich, Essex*

Runner Up

What it Means to be Born Free

Trunk in her mouth, black bristles on her grey skin,
Ears larger than her head,
Rubbing against her mother's leg, in the Savannah.

Soft and clumsy, black beaks and bodies,
White bibs, white dots and white stripes.
Scrabbling behind their white, black and ginger Mother,
As she struts to the lake.
Now and again one will flap its wing stubs.

Silver-grey scattering droplets, streamlined and muscular,
Powering up to the surface, they leap for pure joy.
Mother and baby leap, spinning and turning.
They dive down into the ocean.
Dorsal fins slicing through the water.
Whistles and clicks and echolocation.

Morgan Joy Ashby, *Aberdeen, Scotland*

Morgan Joy Ashby, *Aberdeen, Scotland*

Highly Commended

My Friend Rhino

I left our rhino in the rain;
All night he's been outside
The rain has soaked him to the bone,
Right through his rhino hide.

He's my responsibility.
My folks said, "Don't forget…"
But somehow I neglected him,
And now he's soaking wet.

And both my folks are all upset
And feel I can't be trusted.
I left our rhino in the rain,
And he rhinocerusted.

Sinesipho Wali, *Hendrik Kanise Combined School,*
Alicedale, South Africa

Other Year 8 Poems and Drawings

The Mysteries of the Animal Kingdom

A rustle in the undergrowth,
A blur high up in the tree,
Open your eyes and ears,
Because the world is a mystery.
The mystery of partnership,
Of hope and scarce food,
How animals keep on going,
To bring survival to their brood.
How instinctive and hygienic,
How clever they all are,
They follow their family's traditions,
And travel oh so far.
They care for their habitat,
Each corner and each ditch,
Yet humans are so cruel to them,
And litter lots of rubbish.
Who can swim the best?
A human? Nope, a fish,
But few people care for it,
So soon it could vanish.
A fox, a frog, a fruit bat,
A rhino and a lynx,
All need a perfect environment,
It's easier than one thinks.
Why should animals be killed,
For sport, for food, or fur?

Be a vegetarian,
Because that they would prefer.
Please love animals, pets or in the wild,
Please care for animals, adult or child.

Anya Ormrod Davis, *Chichester, West Sussex*

Anya Ormrod Davis, *Chichester, West Sussex*

127

The First Time

I feel the sandy plains beneath my feet as I run
The dying heat of the setting sun
Never before have I seen a giraffe
Or heard the hyenas laugh
The taste of fresh caught meat
Stays on my tongue as more lions I meet
The distinctive smell of my brand new home
Gives me a place to rest my aching toes
And as I slip into a peaceful sleep
I see the antelope leap
My new pride whisper good night and now I will sleep tight
Under the Acacia tree I am born free.

Isobel Turner, *Heathfield, East Sussex*

Isobel Turner, *Heathfield, East Sussex*

Leopard by Morgan Joy Ashby, *Aberdeen, Scotland*

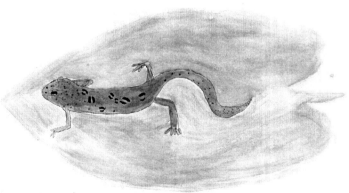

Newt by Morgan Joy Ashby, *Aberdeen, Scotland*

Baby Monkey by Morgan Joy Ashby, *Aberdeen, Scotland*

Year 9

Poems judged by Pam Ayres MBE

Photograph ©Trevor Leighton

Pam Ayres has been a writer, broadcaster and entertainer for almost forty years, and is one of the few authors who has had books in the *Sunday Times* bestseller charts in almost every decade since the 1970s. She is the author of several best-selling poetry collections, including *The Works*, *With These Hands* and *Surgically Enhanced*. Many of her poems are in school textbooks around the world including the UK, USA, China, Australia, New Zealand, The Netherlands, South Africa, Ireland and Singapore.

Funny and approachable, Pam Ayres' poetry sounds simple, as though dashed off, but this is deceptive. Her hair-trigger timing, her eye for the detail of everyday life and for the absurdity therein, makes for an art that hides art.

Pam is one of the most popular female comedians in UK theatres, with annual tours selling out every theatre that she plays. She has toured Australia and New Zealand regularly for over thirty-five years, and is one of the few solo comediennes to have performed in the Concert Hall of the Sydney Opera House. She has performed on several occasions for HM The Queen, and in 2004 was awarded the MBE in the Queen's Birthday Honours.

We were simply delighted when Pam Ayres agreed to judge the oldest of the year groups in this competition. We received far fewer entries in the older groups, but the shortfall in quantity was more than made up for in quality! And in this group all the poems that made the final selection for the book get a special mention by our judge.

This is what Pam had to say:

I chose as my winner *My Leopard* by Juliette Fraser. This beautiful poem made me cry. I could vividly see every scene Juliette described. A wonderfully skilled account of desperate loss. Great economy of words to produce perfect imagery. In particular the lines: "A rose of blood blossoming on her spotted chest," and "Light fading from her golden eyes."

A brilliant poem. Many congratulations to Juliette.

And my runner up was *Rainforest* by Dominik Reynolds. A richly descriptive plea for all that is priceless and in danger. Great atmospheric writing conjuring up the green secrecy, stealth and sounds of a rainforest.

I particularly like the clever insertion of the word "tyre" because by using that small word Dominik introduces all the massive vehicles of destruction. "For under foot and tyre, the forests are falling."

And I simply had to give special mention to *An Elephant's Shadow* by Grace Devereux for its tremendous use of language. This poem brings home the heartlessness and horror of what is happening to our elephants and underlines the shock and disbelief felt by all who love them. Grace's choice of words for the unspeakably sad last verse is very good indeed: Tracked, trailed; Stalked, snared; Maimed, mutilated; Murdered.

This says it all Grace. Well written indeed.

And another wonderful poem is *The Animals' Tea Party* by Amelia Errington because this is a charming and funny poem. I especially liked the line: "Tea was spat in raw disgust." Very descriptive indeed. A lovely poem topped off by a great truism at the end.

I loved the optimism and joy of *Rainforest Life* by Izzy Geatches, which gives us a wonderful picture of all the interlocking fragments of our miraculous wildlife, both tiny and enormous. I liked the rainforest being "a luscious metropolis".

Finally in *Deep in the Wild* by Nisha Nagaraj, I would like to draw attention to the following lines: "To hang ornately across a door" which emphasises the pointlessness of the cruelty. To take so much and do so little with it. "Leave hearts beating amongst the trees." This brings home the horror and brutality of what is happening to our beautiful animals.

I was delighted and enthralled by all this work. I think the future of poetry is in safe hands!

With best wishes to everyone who entered the competition!

Year 9 Winning Poem

My Leopard

Piercing blue eyes,
Dark spotted coat,
Desperate mewling calls,
That was how I found her, under the acacia tree.

Late night feeds,
A spot at the end of my bed,
Playing all day,
That was how I loved her.

Long walks by the dusty road,
Chasing mice,
Climbing trees,
That was how I raised her.

Falling in slow motion,
A rose of blood blossoming on her spotted chest,
Guns lowering,
That was when they shot her.

Beautiful head bowed low,
Light fading from her golden eyes,
Making not a sound,
That was how I lost her.

Surrounded by the sounds of the African bush,
Far away from my house,
In the cool shade,
That was where I buried her, under the acacia tree.

Long sleepless nights,
Weary days,
And an aching heart,
That is how I miss her.

Juliette Fraser, *Tonbridge, Kent*

Juliette Fraser, *Tonbridge, Kent*

Runner Up

Rainforest

Such a vast expanse of mysterious lands
A world not found, a book unopened,
A place where peace remains, where no prints lie, but
The prints of hidden creatures who creep in the shadows,
Unseen.

Howler monkeys swing through silent trees,
Insects wander over endless untrodden ground,
A toucan sings out, voice echoing through the mystical
    forests,
But all these glorious things remain in the shadows,
Unheard.

Luscious shrubbery grows in uncharted numbers, feeding
All the countless species who call the forests home,
Creatures in harmony with a pristine world,
Which shall never be explored, shall always stay
Unseen.

A jaguar stalks through the bushes, its mind clear of any
    thoughts,
For the forest is hushed, no foreign activity interrupting
The natural balance, the undisturbed peace, where
The joyful songs of nature are never heard by man, the
    singers remaining
Untouched.

But no more do the secrets of these lands stay hidden,
For under foot and tyre, the forests are falling,
Saws burn and tear through chapters of the forests history,
Eradicating the beautiful creatures who have always stayed
Unseen.

Loggers must stop, stop the rainforest's one way ticket
To destruction, and they must save the forests,
For there is so much to learn, so much to be cherished,
So much life in the trees that should be left, to remain
    and thrive,
Unseen.

Dominik Reynolds, *Southampton, Hampshire*

Dominik Reynolds, *Southampton, Hampshire*

Highly Commended

An Elephant's Shadow

Lying there in red-stained dust,
They left me there for dead
And pain was my mind's only focus.

These crimson scars will be the reminder,
Everything dreaded, everything feared.
My scars can only show a human's cruelty.

You recognised my panic, you recognised my fear,
I won't forget how you left me for dead.
And I will remember how you only care to harvest.

I remember how the blade glinted in the sun,
How you hacked at my tusk,
And how my dignity was stolen.

You are watching and waiting for another,
Will you leave them for dead too?
To reap the benefits of your exertion.

You feel no heavy burden,
No guilt endured for poaching,
Is our existence so terrible?

Tracked, trailed
Stalked, snared,
Maimed, mutilated,
Murdered.

Who knew death could take a form.

Grace Devereux, *London*

The Animals' Tea Party

It was at the Animals' Tea Party,
When the Elephant declared,
"I'm the finest animal in the land!"
And his reasons why were shared:

"My trunk is long and beautiful,
My tusks are gleaming white,
My eyelashes are long and lush,
And do please note my height!"

Tea was spat in raw disgust,
As the arguments began,
"You?" protested the Giraffe,
"The finest in the land?!"

"I," she started, and looked around,
"Have an air of natural grace,
Have you seen my graceful neck?
Or gazed upon my face?"

The Lion roared, and silence spread,
As he began to speak,
"You might have looks," he told them all,
"But compared to me you're weak,"

"For I'm the strongest in the land,
The feared King of the Jungle,
But before he could say any more,
There was a distant rumble.

Kangaroo hopped along and cried,
"The strongest? I think not!
I possess the greatest strength,
Just observe my mighty hop!"

As Kangaroo took to the air, the wise old owl did say,
"We're all fine, strong and beautiful, just in our own
    special way."

Amelia Errington, *Stroud, Gloucestershire*

Amelia Errington, *Stroud, Gloucestershire*

Rainforest Life

I sit upon my comfortable nest,
Whilst stretching my wonderful wings,
For I must have been blessed,
To be surrounded by such amazing things,

The rainforest is a luscious metropolis,
With so many different species,
There are animals that take predominance,
But also animals that are loud or sleepy,

Animals that are big and small,
Some have beautiful fur or feathers,
Or maybe are very very tall,
But we are all very clever.

I love the unique weather,
As well as the stunning plants,
It's what keeps us altogether,
Even the smallest ants.

You see we are all family,
And always work together,
It must work as we all live happily,
And I'm sure we will do forever.

Izzy Geatches, *Bury St Edmunds, Suffolk*

Deep in the Wild

Deep in the wild, beasts roam free,
From the birds to the bees,
We must not shoot them to the floor,
To hang ornately across a door,
Leave hearts beating amongst the trees.

They have no say, but days ago
The creatures were free to hunt and roam.
Hear the dirge of crying beasts
Deep in the wild.

The cruelty of man does not agree,
But can you hear their desperate plea?
Fight for every fur and claw;
Fight to end this callous war!
Let the beasts roam free,
Deep in the wild.

Nisha Nagaraj, *St Albans, Hertfordshire*

The Mighty Predator by Sajani Jayathma Senanayake,
Colombo, Sri Lanka

Index

*(Page numbers in **bold type** refer to illustrations)*

Other books by Paws n Claws that help wild animals

Paws n Claws Publishing specialises in fictional books about animals and every book makes a donation to the Born Free Foundation.

To find out more about us visit our website:
www.pawsnclawspublishing.co.uk

To find out more about The Jet-Set and to sign up for our fun animal newsletter visit: *www.thejet-set.com*

If you want to learn about the Born Free Foundation and their WildcreW children's club visit:
www.bornfree.org.uk/wildcrew

The Wild n Free Series

Collections of Short Stories by Children aged 9–16.
Winners and runners up from the Paws Animal Writing
Competition for Children

ISBN
978-0-9568939-4-9

ISBN
978-0-9568939-6-3

ISBN
978-0-9568939-7-0

Order from Amazon, other online retailers and from
local bookshops

Royalties to Born Free

Other Books You Might Enjoy

Tonight the Moon is Red

Virginia McKenna

A highly personal collection of poems written by Virginia McKenna, the star of Born Free, recollecting the people, places and animals that have inspired her.

Virginia's great passion and love of poetry is explored in this moving collection of verse, beautifully illustrated by Alex Whitworth.

Published by Muswell Press, 2014

'Every poem challenges, many hurt us – as they should. We flinch with her at the cruelty and exploitation of innocence, of beauty. We weep with her at the loss and the suffering and the longing. Yet we can feel, as she does, through it all, the hope and the beauty and the essential goodness in man and we can rejoice with her in this conviction. She has fought the good fight and these are her battle cries'.

Michael Morpurgo

Copies of the book can be purchased for £9 from the Born Free Foundation's online shop – give.bornfree.org.uk

Gentle Footprints

Edited by Debz Hobbs-Wyatt – *For adults*

Animal Short Stories (but written for adults so this book contains some adult language)

Gentle Footprints is a wonderful collection of short stories about wild animals. The stories are fictional but each story gives a real sense of the wildness of the animal, true to the Born Free edict that animals should be born free and should live free. The animals range from the octopus to the elephant, each story beautifully written.

Gentle Footprints includes a new and highly original story by Richard Adams, author of *Watership Down*, and a foreword by the founder of Born Free, Virginia McKenna OBE.

£1 from the sale of each copy, plus a percentage of the author royalties, will be donated to the Born Free Foundation.

As featured on Mariella Frostrup's Book Show at Hay, 2010 and on ITV's *Loose Women*
ISBN 978-1-907335-04-4

Order from Amazon, bookshops or
www.bridgehousepublishing.co.uk

Lightning Source UK Ltd.
Milton Keynes UK
UKOW04f2035281114

242365UK00002B/31/P